Teaching in the Congregation

PAUL M. LEDERACH

HERALD PRESS
Scottdale, Pennsylvania
Kitchener, Ontario

TEACHING IN THE CONGREGATION

Published by Herald Press, Scottdale, Pa. 15683
Released simultaneously in Canada by Herald Press,
Kitchener, Ont. N2G 4M5
Library of Congress Catalog Card Number: 79-83594
International Standard Book Number: 0-8361-1886-3
Printed in the United States of America
Illustrations and cover art by Elmore Byler
Design: Alice B. Shetler

15 14 13 12 11 10 9 8 7 6 5 4 3 2 1

Distributed overseas by Mennonite Broadcasts, Inc.,
Box 1252, Harrisonburg, Va. 22801

CONTENTS

PREFACE

The proclamation of the gospel resulting in new congregations lies at the heart of the missionary task. Evangelism has had a high priority among many of our churches. However, making disciples must also be coupled with teaching all that Jesus commanded. To emphasize one aspect of Jesus' commission at the expense of the other (whether making disciples or teaching) is to endanger both the growth and the health of the church.

Much has been written on evangelism, personal witnessing, and growth that is useful to young churches. Little, however, has been written to encourage these churches to think deeply about and to plan for adequate teaching. As a result believers are not growing toward maturity as they should. Further, leaders with a thorough knowledge of the Bible and an understanding of the church are not emerging in sufficient numbers to meet the needs of the churches.

This booklet is written to help church leaders think about the place of teaching in the congregation. When the congregation functions as its Lord intended, then its very life will contribute much to effective teaching/learning. Some of these characteristics of congregational life and their implications for teaching are developed in the first part of the book. The latter part examines both the content and the method of teaching that are found in the New Testament.

Teaching in the Congregation provides an elementary, Bible based approach to church education, written especially for congregations with an Anabaptist/Mennonite theological stance.

—Paul M. Lederach

1

FOLLOWING OUR LORD

The Commission of Jesus

TEACHING in the church is rooted in the commission of our Lord (Matthew 28:18-20). He told His followers to *make disciples* of all nations, and to *teach them all that He commanded*. Thus, Christians teach in obedience to Jesus, who has been given all authority in heaven and in earth and who is with His church always.

During the early ministry of Paul, teaching about *the Way* took place in the temple and/or in synagogues. Then, as the church grew, teaching moved into the congregation. Whenever and wherever Christians gathered, teaching took place.

In the early church believers taught what they understood their Lord to be calling them to be and to do in the world. Then, as now, such teaching grew out of their understanding of how brothers and sisters walk in the Spirit (Galatians 5:25), of how they prepare one another for ministry (Ephesians 4:12), and of how they share the faith with both young and old.

The teaching and nurture of Christians within the church is known as the church's teaching ministry.

The Church Gathers and Scatters

The congregation lives both as a "gathered" community and as a "scattered" community.

When the congregation is "gathered," believers worship as a body. They study the Bible together. They pray together. They listen to each other so they can relate their Christian living to the needs of the world. When the congregation is gathered, Christians prepare one another to live as followers of Jesus when they are scattered. Teaching in the congregation helps members to witness and serve in the world, to confess Jesus as Lord in the decisions of life, and to do deeds of loving service. The Lord Jesus does not ask Christians to withdraw from the world; rather He sends them into the world (John 20:21).

When the congregation is "scattered," believers are faced with questions calling for decision and action. These include: how to use wealth and spare time, how to choose standards of living, and how to be good citizens. They must decide how to minister to the needs of others "in the name of Christ"; how to confront oppression, injustice, and violence; and how to function on the job and live at home in ways that can indeed be called Christian. Every congregation has the rhythm of gathering and scattering. Between the *two there is constant interplay.* What is done when the congregation gathers has bearing on what is done when the congregation scatters. Obviously, the teaching ministry of the congregation relates to both gathering and scattering.

Relationships Among Believers

The New Testament goes to great lengths to describe the quality of life in the congregation. Teaching in the early church took place in community. The New Testament describes these personal relationships in many ways. Believers constantly interacted with each other. They valued getting along with other believers in the church, with their families, and with their neighbors. Members submitted to one another and considered themselves members one of another (Romans 12:5). They expressed their love for one another (John 13:34, 35; 1 Thessalonians 3:12). One member edified another (Romans 14:19); they instructed each other (Romans 15:14). They cared for one another (1 Corinthians 12:25). They served one another (Galatians 5:13). Members were subject to one another (Ephesians 5:21). They taught each other (Colossians 3:16). They comforted one another (1 Thessalonians 4:18) and bore each other's burdens (Galatians 6:2). They confessed their faults and prayed for each other (James

5:16). They enjoyed fellowship with one another (1 John 1:7) and showed hospitality one to another (1 Peter 4:9).

People Are More Important Than Organization

In the early church there was much interaction among members. The teaching ministry, like every other work of the congregation, rested more on relationships between people than upon set forms. Human beings do need organizations and institutions so they can use their energies to do things they could not do alone. This is part of being human. People who are growing in their understanding of the meaning of the gospel and of ways to obey our Lord find that personal relationships are very important.

Both the truth of the gospel and the relationships of faith must be demonstrated in each congregation. Clearly, structures are necessary, but relationships among members are of greater importance. To illustrate, a congregation may have a well-organized Sunday school that meets regularly and uses suitable study materials. If, however, the members of the congregation are quarreling and at the point of division, they are not demonstrating the gospel. Teachings about reconciliation, about how hostility ends at the cross, about love and concern for brethren, and about truthfulness are lost in conflict. A quarreling congregation is scarcely a force for the gospel in the world. For who will take seriously the claims of the church for the gospel, if it does not live out these claims? Churches often fail as witnesses to the world because they fail to be communities of love which demonstrate the gospel in both word and example.

The structures agreed upon by the congregation may contribute to good working relationships. However these structures should result from people and their gifts and the work to be done. Too often the congregation is seen as having structures fitted or forced to work. To reapply a Bible teaching—structures are made for people, not people for structures! It is important that structures be kept flexible, permitting new forms to emerge in the light of gifts and needs. In North American congregations so much energy has gone into promoting teaching structures, that little energy is left to seek new forms of teaching. This may also hinder new forms from emerging, either out of a new vision of mission, or from gifts of the Spirit, or from newly identified needs.

When congregations are thriving, moving, living bodies, it is hard to determine the form the teaching ministry will take. It is possible to say, "This is how it was," without being critical of the past. It is possible to say "This is how it is done now in North America" (or in Africa, or in the Near East, or in the Orient) without saying that this is the way it should be done everywhere. Congregations in each geographical area have the responsibility to look, to listen, and to respond obediently to what the Lord is calling them to do. The future depends much upon seeking and obeying God's will in the present.

2

THE NATURE OF THE TEACHING MINISTRY

TEACHING in the congregation takes different forms in different places. However, congregations that take teaching seriously will want their teaching ministry based on sound principles. The teaching ministry and supporting study materials should reflect the following insights:

1. *The teaching ministry serves the life of the congregation.* Teaching is not an end in itself. Nor is it a function separate from or parallel to the life of the congregation (like "Sunday school *and* Church"). The teaching ministry prepares persons to take full part in the life and mission of the church. Therefore, the gathering for *worship and teaching* and the scattering for *witness and*

service are closely related.

2. *The teaching ministry assumes that the gospel has something to say to all of life.* Therefore, the teaching ministry is broad enough to address the needs of all the believers. While it deals with how to understand the Bible, it also relates biblical truths to problems like war, poverty, race, as well as to a wide range of personal concerns.

3. *The teaching ministry and evangelism have a God-given unity.* Therefore, teaching and evangelism must not be made rivals, for both communicate the gospel! The gospel may come to one person as a word that leads to *conversion*—to conviction of sin, to repentance, and to faith. To another person it may come as a word of edification (teaching) that leads to *growth* in Christlikeness. Evangelism and teaching need each other. Any congregation that stresses one without the other is disobedient. Further, both new life in Christ and growth in being like Christ are dependent upon the presence and work of the Holy Spirit. Both teaching and evangelism must, therefore, take place within the community of believers.

4. *The teaching ministry prepares members of the congregation for decision and action.* Learning takes place in a congregation when members test one another, correct one another, and help one another to understand the problems of life in the light of God's Word. Too often the teaching sessions follow a rigid time schedule with too little time for good development and discussion of the subject. As a result, the group may be at a

point of decision when the bell rings. Everything is then dropped, and seldom, if ever, taken up again in the same way.

5. *The teaching ministry helps make clear how the church and the world are related.* In the past, Christians spoke much of being "not of the world." Today Christians see more clearly that they are indeed "in the world." However, now they need help to keep from being "squeezed into the patterns of the world," to maintain their purity, honesty, and separateness. Christians are the salt and light in the world, but need to remember that at any given moment they are overcoming the world or being overcome by the world. The teaching ministry must make Christians able to attack evil as well as to flee from it.

6. *The teaching ministry serves persons of all ages in the congregation.* Children, youth, and adults must all be ministered to, each group on its own level. Such a balanced teaching program responds to the needs of all persons at every stage of growth.

7. *The teaching ministry is flexible.* In North America we have many teaching activities like Sunday school, summer Bible school, boys' club, and girls' club. These have tended to divide the teaching ministry into separate parts. In addition, these teaching activities often become fixed and hard to change. Further, congregations have found it difficult to coördinate their many teaching activities toward the same goal, because no one has an overall view.

Flexibility allows a congregation to develop a teaching ministry that meets its need at any given moment. This requires studying the situation and the work to be done; evaluating resources; and then developing ways to carry out the Lord's command to teach. Flexibility encourages a congregation to consider the problems and needs it faces and a variety of solutions to meet them. More and more persons are asking, What does God want in our congregation? What resources do we have? What must we teach to carry out the Lord's command? How can we best do this? How can we provide teaching for all the needs of all the people so that all may grow together in unity in Christ?

3

THE CONGREGATION, A LEARNING COMMUNITY

PLANNING for teaching in the congregation must be done in the light of the New Testament, in the light of the culture in which the church lives, in the light of history, and in the light of present needs.

Teaching programs should not cause divisions or tensions—between Sunday school *and* church, between the lay *and* the ordained, between teaching *and* evangelism, between teaching *and* worship, and between evangelism *and* discipline.

Each congregation has among its members persons with gifts and skills, whose lives are patterned after Jesus Christ. Such persons should be involved in teaching. Every congregation also has many events and activities which teach.

It is important to identify the learnings these events and activities provide. The following list is intended to illustrate some of these:

Preaching. Learning: the meaning of the Bible and how to interpret it; the story of faith is retold.

Funerals. Learning: the uncertainty and brevity of life; the need to prepare for death; the hope of the Christian beyond death.

Weddings. Learning: what the the Bible says about men, women and marriage; relationships between the home and the congregation; the importance and nature of the Christian home.

Baptism. Learning: the nature of the church; how to enter the church of Jesus Christ.

Foot washing. Learning: the humility and love members need to serve one another.

Communion. Learning: the unity among members of Christ's church; a reminder of Jesus' death; and a forward look to His return.

Mutual aid. Learning: how members care one for another and support each other.

Prayer. Learning: how to talk with God; what to say; when prayers are answered the congregation is strengthened.

Business meetings. Learning: the importance of consulting together; discerning God's will; making decisions.

A wide variety of activities, settings, and persons are available to the congregation for teaching. Each congregation has many opportunities to discover new ways to teach and to think about how its many teaching activities can enrich its total life and mission in the world. The Sunday school has been the place most used for teaching in many parts of the worldwide church. The word "school" has tempted the church to look to the public school for patterns of education. However, patterns for teaching in the congregation should come from an awareness of the nature of the congregation when it functions as Jesus intended.

In the paragraphs that follow are sixteen aspects of the congregation that make it a learning community. From these it becomes clear that the congregation is quite different from the public school and from other organizations in which teaching and learning also take place.

1. *The congregation is a community of new life.*[1] Jesus said, "Truly, truly, I say to you, unless one is born anew, he cannot see the kingdom of God" (John 3:3). The concept of "new birth" suggests "new life." John 3:3 teaches that *new birth* leads to both a *new family* and a *new citizenship* in the kingdom of God. Later, Jesus spoke about the life He gives as an *abundant life.* "I came that they may have life, and have it abundantly" (John 10:10).

Paul makes the point that believers were once dead in trespasses and sins. They followed the prince of the power of the air. They lived in the passions of the flesh, and as a result, they were children of wrath. But God, who is rich in mercy, out of His great love made them alive together with Christ. By grace He saved them and raised them with Christ to sit with them in heavenly places (paraphrase, Ephesians 2:1-6). In the believer's church, children are thought to be spiritually safe until they become aware of and responsible to accept Christ's saving work.)[2]

The point is simply this. Believers were once dead in sin, but now in Jesus Christ they are alive! Jesus brings the community of new life into existence, not physical birth or national citizenship. To receive the *new life*, Jesus said, is to be "born of the Spirit." The new life is *eternal life*, which is the life of God Himself. A community made up of persons with new life certainly sets the congregation apart from every other teaching/learning community.[3]

2. *The congregation is a community of love.* Jesus said, "By this all men will know that you are my disciples, if you have love for one another" (John 13:35). John wrote, "Perfect love casts out fear" (1 John 4:18).

Love is the primary relationship within the community of new life. Loving relationships are important in both teaching and learning.

3. *The congregation accepts the Bible as the Word of God.* This makes the congregation different from other educational contexts. The Bible grew out of community—out of Israel and out of the church. At the same time the Bible brings people into community as it points persons to Jesus Christ. The authority of the Bible is recognized by this community, which sees the Bible as inspired by the Holy Spirit. The community, the church, chose from the many religious writings the books that have continuing authority for the life of the people of God. Therefore, the Bible becomes very important to hear, study, and obey. It corrects the church.

The Bible tells the story of God and His people, of God's revelation, and of human responses to His revelation. This story is told in many ways through history, poetry, proverb, drama. It is told by prophets and apostles. It is interpreted by teaching, by commands, by promises, and by suggestions. The basic thread is the story.

The Bible is the history of God's activity which takes place in time and space. It's a history of the people of God, recording their faithfulness and unfaithfulness, and of God's faithfulness, love, and judgment. Though the Bible contains both the Old and New Testaments, both are accepted as the Word of God. The New Testament is fully and completely authoritative. The revelation under the Old was incomplete, a type and shadow of the full revelation that would come in Jesus Christ and the apostles. However, without an understanding of the Old Testament, it is difficult to understand the New. At the same time a knowledge of the New helps to interpret the Old.

The Bible is the book of the community. It has something to say about all aspects of congregational life. The Bible calls for obedience to God and His will as revealed in Jesus Christ. The community approaches the Scriptures with a spirit of openness and readiness to obey.

4. *The congregation is a community of peace.*[4] The gospel is a gospel of peace (Acts 10:36; Ephesians 6:15). Too often peace has been interpreted as primarily inner peace or the peace of a cleansed conscience. Peace among people is overlooked. "Peace" appears more than 100

times in the New Testament. It has its roots in the Old Testament concept of shalom. God is a God of peace; Jesus is the Lord of peace; and the Holy Spirit gives peace. Peace suggests wholeness and harmony between God and His people, and among His people. The people of God live in harmony within groups and between groups.

In Ephesians 2, Paul deals explicitly with the question of creating peace between humans in conflict. Paul makes clear that Jesus destroys enmity and prejudice, the barriers which create conflict.

The world's way of dealing with conflict is to remove or eliminate the enemy. Differences are dealt with on a win/lose basis. The losers are made to feel second class while holding resentment in the conscious or subconscious mind. The winners feel superior believing their victory declares them right. Jesus has provided a new way for believers to deal with conflict among them.

Jesus made peace by suffering and death, not by vengeance and domination. In Jesus' way of dealing with conflict, persons are not victims or winners, second class or first class, inferior or superior persons. Rather, Jesus creates in Himself one new man—thus making peace. In other words, He helps believers handle conflict so that together they form a dwelling place for the Spirit.

Christians are called to be peacemakers who deal with the things that cause division and hostility. Peacemakers begin at the point of conflict and go to the root of the problem. They refuse to tolerate division or hostility and avoid trying to balance one party against another. The community of peace considers the common existence all believers have in Jesus Christ, not their position or role in a conflict. Among the followers of Jesus, long-suffering, concern, and reconciliation replace personal and social hostility and division. They establish peace and overcome conflicts, not by domination and power, but by following the way of the cross. This is both message and way of life.

5. *The congregation is a worshiping community.*[5] There is no single word in the New Testament for worship. An important one is similar to "liturgy"[6] which means cultic service or ritual. Another word[7] has the meaning of obeisance, to bow low or prostrate oneself.

In the Bible *worship is to exalt and to obey God.* Worship is *offered* (Hebrews 12:28). It may take these forms:

a. *Ceremonial.* In the Old Testament this included sacrifices and dancing. In the New it included speaking, singing, fellowship, and admonishing one another.

b. *Service.* Service to God involves hearing God's Word and responding in a life of loving obedience. In Romans 12:1 Paul speaks of believers offering their lives to God as "a living sacrifice."[8] Micah, a forerunner of New Testament understandings, spoke about the Lord requiring not sacrifice, but justice, mercy, and a humble walk (Micah 6:8).

This view of worship contrasts sharply with views of our times. Worship is frequently thought to be a form of meditation and devotion, basically a private matter between a person and God. Another view holds that the worshiper is to be "inspired." Sometimes people say about a worship service, "I didn't get anything out of it!" To say this is to miss the point completely! In worship one *offers* praise and thanksgiving to God. The worshiper cannot expect to be entertained!

In the Bible, worship is primarily the *function of a group of people*. God is not a private God. He does not belong "to me," like an idol. Jesus taught His followers to pray "Our Father." Thus believers pray in, with, and for the body of Christ. Private worship—prayer, Bible study, and meditation—is also important. However, current tendencies to make worship a private affair and to emphasize emotional feelings need to be balanced with attention to group study and worship. In corporate worship and fellowship many learnings emerge:

(1) As believers come into the presence of God together, they learn who they are as a people and what it means to be united in Christ. Thus they receive a new *sense of identity*. Persons take on the identity of the group with which they are closely related.

(2) Through group worship and interaction believers help each other be *more faithful disciples*. They discover new dimensions of what it means to follow Jesus as they relate to each other in studying the Bible, and in submitting to one another.

(3) Through corporate worship believers dis-

cover *new meanings of "Jesus is Lord."* Worshipers experience praise, thanksgiving, adoration, and giving. They hear God's Word. Teachers and prophets dialogue with the members of the congregation. Out of this comes discernment (1 Corinthians 14:14-33).

In the congregation children and adults worship together. It is very important that children worship with adults. Children's church, a practice common in North America, is not recommended. Too often children's church tends to emphasize a childish theology which distorts the gospel by stressing God's love more than His justice; by stressing His mercy more than His judgment; and by focusing on objects of nature more than upon God's acts in history. Often leaders stress God's acceptance and ignore both His call for repentance and His offer of forgiveness. Finally, relationships and life in the biological family are stressed, while life in the spiritual family, the church, is often overlooked.

Can children actually experience church if they regularly worship by themselves? The believers' church is made up of adults mature enough to say "yes" or "no" to God, and able to accept the results of their decisions. As children worship with adults, they learn the great realities of the Christian faith by observing the examples of discipleship that adults provide.

The worshiping community is in many ways similar to political gatherings. There the participants promote their party and try to get their candidate elected. When their candidate is elected, note the rejoicing! In a similar way the worshiping community is committed to extending the rule of Christ. Note, too, the joy in in congregations when persons are won to Christ or when right triumphs. Even in heaven there is joy over a sinner who repents!

6. *The congregation is gifted by the Holy Spirit.*[9] Gifts of the spirit are listed in Ephesians 4 and in 1 Corinthians 12. Ephesians 4 says that the purpose of gifts is to enable members of the congregation to grow to maturity in Christ, no longer blown about by every wind of doctrine.

7. *The congregation is a witnessing community.*[10] The church has a message, called the "good news." Congregations encourage members to witness individually to others. However, the congregation, by its very nature as a community of the Spirit, of new life, of love, and of peace, is an unusual witness in the world. It is, as Jesus said, "The light of the world" (Matthew 5:14)

Witnessing is an adult function. Adults must call adults to discipleship! Jesus srrounded Himself with a group of mature persons who responded to His call, "Follow Me."

8. *The congregation is a community of servants.* In the congregation, members serve one another (1 Corinthians 12:14; 22-26). A theme of the Bible is that the people of God are a kingdom of priests![11] Priests serve through holiness and intercession. As intercessor-servants, believers are *among*, not *over* each other. This kind of example or model is important. In the world, models of exercising lordship and imposing controls are highly important. In the church, models

of servant-intercessors are needed.

It is interesting to see how the mother of the sons of Zebedee asked for positions for her sons, "Command that these two sons of mine may sit, one at your right hand and one at your left, in your kingdom" (Matthew 20:21). Her request illustrates the now popular organizational charts—Jesus at the top and James and John on the next level—one on the right, the other on the left.

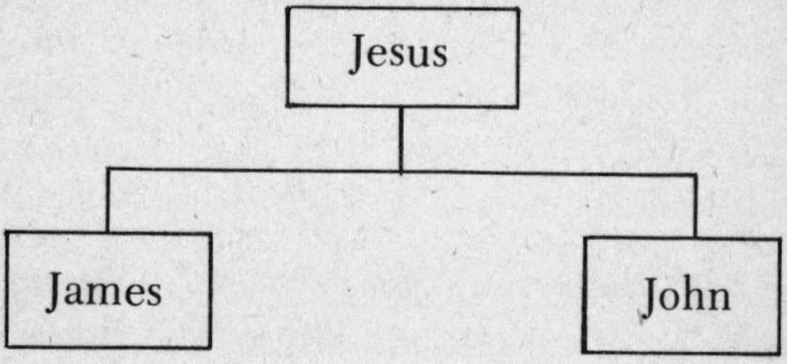

Jesus did not grant the woman's request. He said, "You know that the rulers of the Gentiles lord it over them, and their great men exercise authority over them. It shall not be so among you; but whoever would be great among you must be your servant, and whoever would be first among you must be your slave; even as the Son of man came not to be served but to serve, and to give his life as a ransom for many" (Matthew 20:25-28). Jesus' followers move downward as servants of the Lord and each other in contrast to men of the world who climb upward to positions of power over others. In the congregation greatness is neither in position nor in the opportunity to exercise power. It is in service.

9. *The congregation includes persons of all ages.* Elementary schools have young children, high schools have teenage children, and colleges have young people. Each of these groups represents but a thin slice of the total life-span. The congregation, however, includes all, from the very young to the very old.

In the congregation persons of all ages can contribute to the growth of all. By its very nature the congregation provides unusual opportunities for generations to learn from each other the Christian walk, for relating to Jesus is a lifelong process.

10. *The congregation provides models of discipleship.*[12] Paul said, "Be imitators of me, as I am of Christ" (1 Corinthians 11:1). As a model, Paul did not arrogantly ask others to follow. Rather, he quietly invited others to follow because he was seriously following Jesus and living under His lordship, direction, and judgment. In a similar way, believers provide examples or models of discipleship for others.

11. *The congregation is a disciplined community.*[13] The gospel that wins persons to Jesus Christ also teaches and empowers them to live a life of discipleship. When a congregation engages in reproof and correction, it is taking seriously the same gospel that calls persons to Christ in evangelism. Reproof and correction set in motion powerful forces for teaching and learning.

Discipline, rather than harming congregational life, provides important learnings for all persons in the congregation. The purpose of discipline is the salvation of the individual that has stumbled. At the same time discipline maintains the purity of the life and witness of the congregation. Through discipline all grow more like Jesus Christ, as the fallen are restored and the faithful consider themselves so that they are not tempted.

The pastoral epistles identify some of the problems early congregations dealt with as a disciplined community. Paul, in his first letter to Timothy, instructed him: to rebuke those who try to make godliness a means of gain (1 Timothy 6:5); to deal openly with valid charges against leaders (5:19, 20); to discern the godless myths of their culture that should be rejected (1:4; 4:6, 7); to pray for rulers (2:1, 2); to determine who should serve as leaders (3:1-13), who should be commissioned for special service (4:14), and who should receive mutual aid from the church (5:1-16).

Likely children will learn more about the Christian life by watching members wrestle with issues of morality and relationships than by sitting in a classroom with a teacher and ever-so-well developed curriculum materials.

12. *The congregation has a sense of identity.* This self-awareness grows out of an understanding of the past, the present life, and the future of the people of God, both in this life and the one beyond.

The identity of the people of God is not tied to the nations in which they live. God's people have always been aliens and exiles (1 Peter 2:11). The history of a nation and the history of the people of God follow two different streams. For the people of God the stream of history goes back to Jesus Christ, and thence to Abraham. This is their true heritage and identity. This stream flows to all continents, to all races, and to all languages.

Likely, the identity of God's people springs more from the beliefs and practices they affirm than from any other source. Usually identity comes from outside rather than from within the group because affirmations lead to life and practices that are noticed by others. A group probably cannot establish its own identity. Historically, the identity of God's people has come form the world. At Antioch the followers of Jesus were first called "Christians." Those who committed themselves to adult baptism as a symbol of their relationship to Jesus Christ and His church were called "Anabaptists." The beliefs and practices affirmed in obedience to Christ and the Scriptures create identity. "A city set on a hill cannot be hid" (Matthw 5:14).

13. *The congregation experiences openness and honesty.* Within the community there is a deep awareness that no one is perfect, and that all need God's grace and forgiveness. The natural tendency is to hide from God and from each other. Too often, these tendencies are manifested in the church.

In a community of openness and honesty there is "speaking the truth in love" (Ephesians 4:15). In most groups there is a lot of *speaking,* but in a community of openness and honesty the speaking is *the truth.* False appearances (masks) are removed. And yet, *speaking the truth* is not the goal, for truth can be spoken to hurt others or to satisfy others' curiosity. The goal is to speak the truth *in love*—so that all will grow, in every way, in Jesus Christ.

In a community of openness and honesty, failures as well as successes are shared with brothers and sisters. There is freedom to reveal that one has problems. Fellow believers listen, not merely to satisfy their curiosity, but to help, to confess similar needs, to give and counsel, support, and prayer. In such openness the Holy Spirit works more fully in the lives of all. In a community of openness and honesty, believers sense more clearly the truth of Paul's statement, "But we have this treasure in earthen vessels [our bodies], to show that the transcendent [or supreme] power belongs to God and not to us" (2 Corinthians 4:7).

An environment of openness and honesty encourages learning, for persons are free to experience, to break out of old behaviors and experience new ones. There is no need to cover mistakes, or to put on a false front, because the community gives encouragement, patience, and support.

14. *The congregation is concerned about the families of its members.*[14] The baptized members of the congregation are mature believers. Many members are married and have families. Many are not married. As the world has tended to idolize sex, so the church has tended to idolize family. The church has also overlooked single persons. To be married or to be single has no bearing on the value of a member's contribution

to the life in the congregation. There is only one choice—*discipleship*. Marriage, singleness, or celibacy in a community are ways to express discipleship.

The Apostle Paul made strong statements in support of those who were single (1 Corinthians 7). Therefore, if unmarried adult members of the congregation feel like second-class members, the congregation is being unfaithful.

When planning for family life education in the congregation, this relationship between the congregation and families of members should be kept in view. The congregation is not made strong by attempting to strengthen each family. Rather the New Testament suggests that when the congregation's teaching ministry fulfills the Lord's plan for it, then the families of members are strengthened.

The New Testament does not speak directly to families apart from the congregation. Rather, family living is dealt with first of all in the congregation! All of Paul's concerns for the family were expressed first to congregations. His teaching about husband and wife relations were put in a letter addressed to the Corinthian church. His insights into the love between husband and wife were written to the congregations that received the Ephesian letter.

As issues of family living are dealt with in the congregation, insights and learnings emerge that believers can put into practice at home. Members who are married and have families are free to share problems; they are encouraged and given help by their brothers and sisters in the congregation. Within the members of the congregation—the spiritual family—are found the necessary insights and experiences needed to help families with their problems.

15. *The congregation has rhythms.* There is the rhythm of gathering in the *large assembly* and in the *small group.* (Participation in both is important for each member.) There is the rhythm of *proclamation* (preaching) and *teaching and admonishing* one another. There is the rhythm of *gathering* and *scattering*—gathering to worship and to equip one another for scattering as witnesses and servants in the world.

These rhythms are deeply related. Too often, preaching in the large group follows one theme, then teaching and admonition in the small group follows another. If the themes in the large group and in the small groups are related, they can be discussed in detail and made clear to everyone. Wrong ideas can be corrected and the group can move from passive listening and talking to action.

16. *The congregation is a springboard for God's action in the world.* The congregation lives God's love in the world (Romans 5:5). Paul makes the point that it is *for* the church, and *through* the church, that God is doing His work in the world (Ephesians 1:19-23; 2:9, 10). Further, those who are part of the church are His workmanship, created in Christ Jesus *for good works.*

These sixteen aspects of the congregation as a learning community demonstrate that teaching in the congregation must grow out of its nature and life. As it does so, the teaching ministry will be strengthened and enriched. As these are taken seriously, a teaching ministry will emerge that is true to God's intention. The congregation will avoid copying the weak points of the learning institutions outside of the church, such as the public school. To see the richness and the range of possibilities God has given each congregation for teaching/learning may begin a search for new and more obedient forms of education in the congregation.

4

PUTTING TEACHING MATERIALS TO WORK

SOME persons in overseas churches may see teaching materials as *the* key to an effective teaching ministry. They say, "If we had curriculum materials, then we could do the job!" At the other extreme are persons in North America who have many study materials for all ages, and yet blame curriculum for their failures! Some of these people say, "If we had curriculum materials *from another publisher*, then we could do the job!"

Both views give to curriculum a role that it cannot fill! *Curriculum materials do not teach themselves.* They are simply tools. Men and women, boys and girls, are needed if teaching/

learning is to take place. Sometimes the best curriculum materials are poorly used. Sometimes the poorest curriculum materials are effectively used by skilled teachers.

In many countries curriculum materials have been written, illustrated, printed, and put on a warehouse shelf. There they stayed. Why? Someone saw the need for curriculum materials, but no one did the equally important work of thinking how the materials were to be used, by whom, with whom, when, and where. Unless the settings in which curriculum materials are to be used are carefully defined and promoted, the materials may go unused. Curriculum materials support the teaching program. Generally, they do not create it.

In summary: (a) curriculum materials are tools for teaching. They support the teaching program. (b) the teaching program should be developed before curriculum materials are created. As the teaching ministry undergirds the congregation in its mission, so curriculum undergirds the teaching ministry.

The Bible and the quality of the life of the congregation are of greater importance than curriculum materials. Each congregation has a purpose and it is important that the congregation perceives its central purpose. Then it can more clearly discern whom it teaches, what it teaches, how it teaches, where it teaches, and when. These issues must be studied before the curriculum materials are produced or chosen.

Thus, curriculum materials will grow out of

the life of the church, its purposes, and its clearly perceived educational needs.

Curriculum materials bring three important dimensions to teaching in the congregation:

1. *Balance.* In a balanced teaching ministry all the elements of the Christian faith receive attention and emphasis—Old Testament/New Testament materials have appropriate emphasis; both content and experience are emphasized; no one aspect of discipleship is stressed while another is scarcely mentioned.

2. *Comprehensiveness.* The learner will study all the content and have all the experiences the church wants to include in its teaching ministry.

3. *Sequence.* Each part of the curriculum is related to what has gone before and to what will follow. The curriculum takes into account the growth and experience of learners. Content, concepts, and experiences will come in an orderly fashion, so that learnings will be connected, and will build on each other.

Curriculum materials provide teachers and students with specific guidance in three areas: (a) information and background understanding, (b) suggestions for procedures, and (c) opportunities for participation.

5

GROUPING FOR TEACHING

LITTLE is recorded in the New Testament about structures for teaching in the early church. The epistles provide a few clues. Organization in the early church seemed to reflect levels of spiritual attainment. Persons were not grouped by age, or by interest in a special topic of study, but by progress in the Christian life!

Hebrews 5:11—6:1 reflects a typical, three-level grouping. There were those who were working with "first principles" (v. 12), those able to "distinguish good from evil" (v. 14), and those who were "perfect"[15] (6:1, KJV). The level of the "perfect" was the goal of Jesus' teaching: "You, therefore, must be perfect, as your heavenly

Father is perfect" (Matthew 5:48). It was the goal for Paul: "Among the mature [perfect] we do impart wisdom" (1 Corinthians 2:6); "In thinking be mature [perfect]" (1 Corinthians 14:20). The goal of the Spirit's gifts is "mature [perfect] manhood" (Ephesians 4:13).

For Paul, to be perfect was basically a process: "Not that I have already obtained this or am already perfect" (Philippians 3:12). Paul had to press on! Those who were of the "perfect" had the same attitude (Philippians 3:15). This was also the view of the preacher in Hebrews, that maturity, or perfection, is a process. To be perfect is to have the ability to make an appropriate response in every situation. In this sense Jesus was perfect. Hebrews 5:8, 9 says that Jesus was in the process of being made perfect. Paul also longed to present every man mature (perfect) in Christ (Colossians 1:28). And Epaphras prayed for the Colossians that they would "stand mature [perfect] and fully assured in all the will of God" (Colossians 4:12).

1 John refers to a three-level grouping: "children," "fathers," "young men." (1 John 2:12-14).

Paul, like the preacher of Hebrews, recognized those who were "infants," "babes," or "children" (1 Corinthians 3:1; 13:11; 14:20; Ephesians 4:14). These were in contrast to those who were "grown men," "mature," or "perfect" (1 Corinthians 2:6; 13:11; 14:20; Ephesians 4:13).

In many respects the levels in the early church followed Jewish practices in which a person was first a "son" (from 13 to 20 years of age), then one who "knew good and evil" (20 years of age and older), and finally "perfect" (those who were married, paid taxes, provided sacrifices, and exercised adult responsibility).

From the history of the period immediately following New Testament days, we know also that there were degrees of initiation—unbaptized novices, baptized trainees, and full members.

Allowing persons of similar age or interest to study together likely has many advantages. When younger, middle age, and older persons study together they can learn from each other. What would happen if congregations put those with similar spiritual growth together for study?

6

UNDERSTANDING THE LEARNING PROCESS

THE most important word for "teacher"[16] in the New Testament means "master of instruction" or "schoolmaster." It refers to one who teaches definite skills like reading or music, or who provides systematic instruction. The Greek word for teacher suggests that the teacher uses a systematic method to communicate what he teaches.

This word for teacher appears 58 times in the New Testament; of 48 uses in the gospels, 41 refer to Jesus! In Acts and the epistles a group of leaders in the Christian community were called "teachers" (Acts 13:1; 1 Corinthians 12:28; Ephesians 4:11).

A teacher generally had a group of disciples.[17] These disciples learned not only from hearing the teacher, but also from observing the teacher's example. It is interesting to note that neither Jesus' disciples nor the leaders in the early church took the name "Master" or "Teacher" for themselves, as did Jesus. However, in the early church, teachers formed an identifiable group of leaders. In 1 Corinthians 12:29 they are listed after the apostles and prophets, and in Ephesians 4:11 after the apostles, prophets, and evangelists. The task of teachers was to lead the congregation to clear understandings of the Word and will of God.

The verb "to teach"[18] and the noun "teacher" have the same root. To teach implied both the knowledge that the teacher was thought to have and the example that the teacher provided. In fact, it was the example of the teacher that provided the bridge for the pupil to move from content to the highest possible personal development.

The verb "to teach"[19] is found 95 times in the New Testament; two thirds of these are in the Gospels and Acts; 10 are in Paul's writings. Generally speaking, teaching was a very prominent feature of Jesus' public ministry. For Him the synagogue and the temple were the places to teach. Luke 4:20 tells how He stood to read the Scripture in the synagogue and then sat down to teach.

At times "to teach" was to present the totality of Christian truth. In Acts 18:11, Paul was in Corinth teaching the Word of God. Apollos taught accurately the things concerning Jesus (Acts 18:25). The last paragraph in Acts tells how Paul was teaching the Lord Jesus Christ (Acts 28:31). To teach in this sense embraced both teaching *about* Jesus and the teachings *of* Jesus. Jesus commissioned His disciples to teach all that He commanded—the total message of His life and words (Matthew 28:20). Paul also used this verb to describe his teaching (Ephesians 4:20; Colossians 2:7; 2 Thessalonians 2:15).

There are several Greek words translated "to learn" in the New Testament. One of these[20] provides the root for the word "disciple."[21] Jesus used this verb frequently—"Take my yoke upon you, and learn from me" (Matthew 11:29). *Learn* the parable of the fig tree (Matthew 24:32). Paul also used it several ways: *learning* Christ (Ephesians 4:20); *learning* to be content (Philippians 4:11); those who are ever *learning*, but never able to come to the knowledge of the truth (2 Timothy 3:7); "But as for you, continue in what you have learned and have firmly believed, knowing from whom you learned it" (2 Timothy 3:14). The preacher said that Jesus *learned* obedience by what He suffered (Hebrews 5:8).

Another Greek word[22] is also translated in a variety of ways: nurture (Ephesians 6:4, KJV); instruction (2 Timothy 3:16, KJV); and chastening (Hebrews 12:5, 7, 8, and 11, KJV). Paul used the verb form[23] when referring to his own educational background, "educated according to the strict manner of the law of our fathers" (Acts 22:3). Paul also wrote to Timothy that opponents were to be corrected (instructed) in gentleness (2 Timothy 2:25). And to Titus he wrote that "the grace of God has appeared . . . *training* us to renounce irreligion and worldly passions" (2:11, 12).

A third word[24] is also translated in a variety of ways, but one of its main meanings has the idea of adjusting. "Every one when he is fully taught will be like his teacher" (Luke 6:40). It is used in 1 Thessalonians 3:10, to supply what is lacking in one's faith. It is found again in Galatians 6:1. Here a fallen brother is to be restored to live as he did before being overcome by sin. This word is in the benediction in Hebrews 13:21, where God is to equip the believer with everything good, to do His will. Paul used this word in his concluding remarks in 2 Corinthians, "Finally, brethren, farewell. Mend [or adjust] your ways" (13:11).

In summary, the New Testament refers frequently to teachers, to teaching, and to learning. Jesus saw Himself as a teacher. There were also teachers in the church. Teaching involved both content and examples. The learner was a follower of a teacher, or a disciple. When fully taught, the learner became like the teacher.

7

TEACHING IN THE EARLY CHURCH

THE content of teaching in the New Testament seems to fall into six areas:

1. *The early church taught the Old Testament.* It was the Bible of the early church. Early Christians studied the Old Testament because it not only pointed to Jesus Christ, but also helped to make clear His Person and work. It is almost impossible to understand all that the New Testament says about Jesus without a knowledge of the Old Testament. Jesus constantly referred to the Old Testament. Many New Testament books, such as Revelation and Hebrews, can scarcely be understood without a good Old Testament background.

2. *The early church studied and repeated the words of Jesus.* Christians today tend to emphasize the birth, death, resurrection, and return of Jesus and to neglect His life and teaching. This imbalance is reflected in the creeds, which skip from "born of the Virgin Mary" to "crucified under Pontius Pilate." The early church avoided this problem by carefully studying the teachings of Jesus. Jesus told His disciples that His words should abide in them (John 15:7). Paul also wrote, "If any one teaches otherwise and does not agree with the sound words of our Lord Jesus Christ and the teaching which accords with godliness, he is puffed up with conceit, he knows nothing" (1 Timothy 6:3, 4).

Paul makes constant allusions to the words of Jesus and Jesus' figures of speech. For example, when Paul met with the Ephesian elders he quoted words of Jesus not found elsewhere, "It is more blessed to give than to receive" (Acts 20:35). The life and words of Jesus are of unequalled importance. They reveal what God is like and also how God intended people to live. It is not an accident that John recorded the words of Peter to Jesus, "You have the words of eternal life" (John 6:68).

3. *The early church taught doctrine.* There are many doctrinal statements in the New Testament. These statements are short and clear. Since many members of the early church could not read and were unlearned, doctrine had to be taught in ways that were easily understood, easily meditated upon, and easily shared.

Here are some examples of doctrinal statements; which were often put in the form of poetry or hymns.

There is one body and one Spirit,
just as you were called to the one hope that belongs
    to your call,
one Lord, one faith, one baptism,
one God and Father of us all, who is above all and
    through all and in all. Ephesians 4:4-6.

Have this mind among yourselves, which is yours
    in Christ Jesus,
who, though he was in the form of God,
did not count equality with God a thing to be
    grasped,
    but emptied himself,
    taking the form of a servant,
    being born in the likeness of men.
And being found in human form
    he humbled himself
and became obedient unto death,
    even death on a cross.
Therefore God has highly exalted him
and bestowed on him the name which is above
    every name,
that at the name of Jesus every knee should bow,
    in heaven and on earth and under the earth,
and every tongue confess that Jesus Christ is Lord,
    to the glory of God the Father.
        Philippians 2:5-11.

For there is one God, and there is one mediator between God and men, the man Christ Jesus, who gave himself as a ransom for all. 1 Timothy 2:5, 6.

Great indeed, we confess, is the mystery of our religion:

He was manifested in the flesh,
vindicated in the Spirit,
  seen by angels [apostles],
preached among the nations,
believed on in the world,
  taken up in glory.
    1 Timothy 3:16.

He reflects the glory of God
and bears the very stamp of his nature,
upholding the universe by his word of power.
    Hebrews 1:3.

Holy, blameless, unstained,
separated from sinners,
exalted above the heavens. Hebrews 7:26.

These passages suggest ways doctrine might be taught today, using brief, pithy statements set in poetic or musical forms.

4. *The early church taught ethics and morality.* One form of moral teaching relates to *stations in life.* Persons in various positions are taught how to behave—for example, as a wife, as a husband, as children, as slaves, or as masters. See Colossians 3:18—4:5 and Ephesians 5:21—6:9.

The epistles contain frequent lists of virtues and vices: the works of the flesh (Galatians 5:19-21), the fruit of the Spirit (Galatians 5:22-24), and a series of virtues and vices (Ephesians 4:25—5:2). In Ephesians 4 the vice is stated first, next the virtue, then a principle for practicing the virtue. For example,

Let the thief no longer steal [vice]
but rather let him labor, doing honest work with his hands [virtue],
so that he may be able to give to those in need [principle]. Ephesians 4:28.

In Ephesians 5:3-14 Paul lists vices, discusses the contrast between light and darkness, and concludes with the baptismal hymn:

Awake, O sleeper,
And arise from the dead,
And Christ shall give you light.

Paul writes of putting to death certain kinds of behavior, of putting away vices, and of "putting on" the new nature. Colossians 3:5-9. The new nature is more fully described in Colossians 3:12, where believers are told to "put on" the Christian virtues. All of these culminate in love, which binds everything together in "perfect harmony." This section concludes with the call to believers to let the Word of Christ dwell in them. It asks believers to teach and admonish one another in all wisdom, in singing of psalms and hymns, and in giving thanks to God.

Other passages containing such lists are:

• 1 Corinthians 6:9-11. Here Paul makes the point that those who practice such vices will not inherit the kingdom of God. He notes that some of these vices had been practiced by believers, but they were washed, sanctified, and justified in the name of Jesus Christ.

• 1 Timothy 1:9-11. Here Paul lists vices contrary to sound doctrine and the gospel of Christ.

• 2 Timothy 2:22. Here Paul warns Timothy of

lusts and lists virtues. In 3:2-5 Paul describes the irreligious behavior of evil men in the last days.

• Titus 3:3. here Paul contrasts the new life in Christ with behavior before the washing of regeneration and renewal in the Holy Spirit.

These lists of virtues and vices, things to "put off" and "put on," are more than simple catalogs. When these lists are compared, it became clear that they were really outlines for the moral teaching of church members. The teaching was specific. Likely each word brought to the mind of the learner definite behaviors to avoid or to practice.

5. *The early church taught how to conduct the life of the congregation.* Many passages in the epistles tell how to conduct business in the congregation: how to select leaders (1 Timothy 3; Titus 1:5-9); how to take care of widows (1 Timothy 5:3-16); how to pay church leaders (1 Timothy 5:17-19); how to handle accusations against church leaders (1 Timothy 5:19-21); how to give (2 Corinthians 8:9; 1 Corinthians 16:2).

6. *The early church taught how to share the faith.* There was much emphasis on making the central confession, "Jesus is Lord" (1 Timothy 6:13, 14). This was not a matter of reciting creeds primarily, for the true disciple sought the meaning of the lordship of Jesus Christ in all of life. He was committed to be obedient to the Lord, so that by word and deed the gospel would be communicated to others.

There are a number of Greek words in the New Testament that seem to embrace all six of these areas, or combinations of them. One of these words is translated "teaching."[25] Sometimes this word is used to refer to the whole of Jesus' teaching, including both His life and His words. At times "teaching" included all of the apostles' teaching (Acts 2:42). At times it stood for the Christian lifestyle.[26] In a negative way, this word is used of the lifestyle of the Pharisees (Matthew 16:12).

Closely connected is a word which suggests the "sum of teaching."[27] This word is most common in the pastoral epistles, with fifteen of the twenty-one usages in the New Testament found there. The word refers to the historical revelation of God as fulfilled in Jesus. At times this word has the sense of "systems of truth." For example, 2 Timothy 3:16 (KJV), where Scripture "is profitable for doctrine."

It should be noted that there are both "true" and "false" systems of teaching. In Ephesians 4:14 Paul wrote about "wind of doctrine." In Colossians 2:22 he refers to "doctrines of men" (KJV). In 1 Timothy 1:10 Paul writes about teachings that are "contrary to sound doctrine," and in 1 Timothy 4:1 he speaks of doctrines or systems of the devils.

A third term that embraces the totality of Christian teaching is "tradition."[28] Sometimes this word is translated "ordinance" in English Bibles. "Tradition," however, is the more frequent. Paul wrote about keeping "traditions" as he delivered them (1 Corinthians 11:2), and about the "tradition that you received from us" (2 Thessalonians 3:6). He admonished the brethren to "stand firm and hold to the traditions which you were taught by us" (2 Thessalonians 2:15). For Paul, the total of Christian teaching is "tradition." It comes from the Lord (1 Corinthians 11:23) and from Paul (1 Corinthians 15:3). What Paul and Jesus taught are in opposition to "human tradition" (Mark 7:8; Colossians 2:8).

In recent times in North America the word "tradition" has come into disrepute. However, for Paul and other New Testament writers there was no conflict between piety and a high estimate of tradition, which meant the totality of Christianity teaching.

There are two other words that refer to the total of Christian teaching. One is found in 1 Timothy 6:20—"What has been entrusted."[29] The sense behind this is "deposit." Christian truth is considered a "good deposit" with which one is entrusted. The second word found in 2 Timothy 1:12-14 is "sound words"[30] which in the Greek means "healthy words." These are to be guarded since they come from the apostle. They are also of Christ Jesus and are entrusted by the Holy Spirit.

In summary, the early Christian church maintained a strong teaching emphasis. Christians studied carefully the Old Testament Scriptures and the teachings of Jesus. They taught doctrine through poetry and music and showed how faith related to one's actions. They also taught how to conduct the life of the congregation and how to share faith with others. The next chapter examines some of the methods the early Christians used in their teaching activities.

8

TRANSMITTING THE TRUTH

THE early church used two methods of teaching within which most teaching and learning activities can be placed; first, passing on or transmitting content; and second, providing a model or example.

Jesus' *words* (content) and His *life* (model) were the teaching. The same was true for Paul. Paul emphasized the content of Christian faith and the need to live it in daily life. "Finally, brethren, whatever is true, whatever is honorable, whatever is just, whatever is pure, whatever is lovely, whatever is gracious, if there is any excellence, if there is anything worthy of praise, think about these things [content]. What you have learned and received and heard and seen in me [model], do; and the God of peace will be with you" (Philippians 4:8, 9). Transmission of content is studied in this chapter, living it in the next.

Both Old and New Testaments emphasize the *transmission* of truth, passing on the faith from person to person, from generation to generation. One form of transmission was to tell the story of the great acts of God and its meaning to His people. There are two well-developed examples of this in the New Testament:

1. The sermon of Stephen in Acts 7. Here the acts of God are traced from Abraham to the death and resurrection of Jesus. Along with telling the events, Stephen also interpreted their meaning.
2. The list of the faithful in Hebrews 11 where the writer cites one example after another of faithful persons.

Two words in the New Testament, "received"[31] and "delivered,"[32] describe the method of transmission. Sometimes these words are found together:

> For I *received* from the Lord what I also *delivered* to you, that the Lord Jesus on the night when he was betrayed took bread (1 Corinthians 11:23).
>
> For I *delivered* to you as of first importance what I also *received* that Christ died for our sins in accordance with the scriptures (1 Corinthians 15:3).

Sometimes Paul used *received* alone. He did not *receive* the gospel from men (Galatians 1:12).

The Philippians *received* instructions from Paul (Philippians 4:9). The Thessalonians *received* the Word of God from Paul (1 Thessalonians 2:13). The Thessalonians also *learned* (or received) from Paul how to live and to please God (1 Thessalonians 4:1). Paul warned about living in idleness which was not in accord with the tradition[33] they *received* from him (2 Thessalonians 3:6).

Paul also used *delivered* alone. For example, in Romans 6:17, KJV, Paul referred to the form of doctrine which was *delivered* you. Luke, in the introduction to his Gospel wrote that he compiled a narrative of the things that happened, "just as they were *delivered* to us by those who from the beginning were eyewitnesses and ministers of the word" (Luke 1:2).

Jude also wrote (verse 3) about the necessity "to contend for the faith which was once for all *delivered* to the saints." And Peter, when writing about those who had fallen away, said that it would have been better for them never to have known the way of righteousness than after knowing it to turn back from the holy commandment *delivered* to them (2 Peter 2:21).

In the New Testament *preaching* is also a form of transmission. Many Greek words in the New Testament are translated by the English word "preach."

One of the more important words translated "to preach"[34] appears about sixty-one times in the New Testament—nine times in Matthew, fourteen times in Mark, nine times in Luke, and eight times in Acts. The underlying meaning of this word "preach" is to be a herald, especially among victors in a contest. Ordinarily, this word does not refer to the delivery of a learned or edifying discourse with well-chosen words and a pleasant voice, rather it refers to the declaration of an event. It should be noted in passing that in John's writings (except for Revelation 5:2) "preach" does not occur. John uses the word "witness" (root for the word martyr)—a witness, rather than a herald's cry!

Sometimes this word "to preach" refers to the essence of the gospel, to *preach* Christ (Acts 8:5) and to the word of faith which we *preach* (Romans 10:8). The center of Paul's message was to *preach* Christ crucified (1 Corinthians 1:23). He told Timothy to *preach* the word (2 Timothy 4:2). The early church believed that divine intervention took place through proclamation.

Another word translated "to preach"[35] has the sense of a solemn, religious message. This word appears eleven times in Acts, and six times in Paul's letters. "They *preached* the word of God" (Acts 13:5, KJV). "Jesus, whom I *preach* unto you" (Acts 17:3, KJV). "The word of God was *preached*" (Acts 17:13, KJV). "They which *preach* the gospel" (1 Corinthians 9:14, KJV). Those who *preach* Christ out of contention (Philippians 1:15). "Whom we *preach*, warning every man" (Colossians 1:28, KJV). The words spoken at the Lord's Supper *preach* Christ (1 Corinthians 11:26). This word is used to bring into focus the unique, historical reality of Jesus.

At times preaching and teaching[36] appear together. For example, "*preaching* the kingdom of God and *teaching* about the Lord Jesus" (Acts 28:31); "You then who *teach* others, will you not teach yourself? While you *preach* against stealing, do you steal?" (Romans 2:21).

It has been observed that preaching tended to occur more in the open, while teaching occurred in the synagogue. Teaching[37] was the exposition of Scripture in the synagogue so that the righteous would increase knowledge. Preaching[38] was the herald's cry in the streets and the villages declaring what God was doing in the midst of His people. But according to Luke 4:21-30 preaching also occurred in the synagogue.

Another word often translated preach[39] refers to the delivery of a religious lecture or sermon. In the KJV this word is frequently translated "disputing." Paul addressed groups in the temple (Acts 24:12), in the school of Tyrannus (Acts 19:9), and in the church at Troas (Acts 20:7, 9).

There is another word translated "preaching."[40] It is frequently used of Jesus, especially in the Book of Luke. It is often used in connection with the mission activity of the apostles in preaching Christ (Acts 5:42). They went everywhere *preaching* the word (Acts 8:4). Philip, in his missionary activities, was *preaching* the things concerning Christ, *preaching* the gospel in many villages, and he *preached Jesus* to the man from Ethiopia (Acts 8:12, 25, 35).

This word had a special mission emphasis. It is used in Acts 14 and 15 in connection with Paul's preaching to the Gentiles. In Romans 10:15 Paul quotes Isaiah, referring to the feet of them that *preach* the gospel of peace and bring glad tidings of good things. To *preach the gospel* (1 Corinthians 1:17) seems to sum up the "whole" activity of the apostles. Just as the prophets of old could scarcely keep from speaking their messages, so Paul felt a divine constraint to preach (1 Corinthians 9:16). Paul wanted to preach the gospel in the regions beyond (2 Corinthians 10:16); he wrote about preaching among the Gentiles (Ephesians 3:8). This word is used in connection with a host of witnesses—disciples, apostles, and evangelists. It means more than speaking. It has the sense of preaching under the full authority and power of God, to proclaim the good news.

It should be noted, too, that the Greek word which means "to speak"[41] is sometimes translated "to preach" (see Mark 2:2; Acts 8:25).

Other words in the New Testament also contribute to an understanding of how faith can be transmitted to others. One of these is "exhort" (beseech):[42] "He testified . . . and *exhorted*" (Acts 2:40); "*exhorting* them to continue" (Acts 14:22); and "*exhorted* the brethren" (Acts 15:32). This word is also translated "beseech" in the King James version. "I *beseech* you therefore, brethren" (Romans 12:1); "now I *beseech* you, brethren" (Romans 15:30); "now I *beseech* you, brethren" (Romans 16:17). See also 1 Corinthians 1:10, 1 Corinthians 16:15, 2 Corinthians 10:1, Ephesians 4:1, and 1 Thessalonians 4:10.

Beseeching and exhorting were done by leaders and also by believers one to another. Exhorting was to be done every day (Hebrews 3:13). Believers were to meet together, "encouraging [exhorting] one another, and all the more as you see the Day drawing near" (Hebrews 10:25).

Another word is "command."[43] Paul wrote: "unto the married I *command*" (1 Corinthians 7:10); "as we *charged* you" (1 Thessalonians 4:11); "do the things which we *command*" (2 Thessalonians 3:4); "we *command* you, brethren" (3:6); "we gave you this *command*" (3:10); "such persons we *command* and exhort" (3:12); "*command* and teach these things" (1 Timothy 4:11); and "*command* this" (1 Timothy 5:7). "I *charge* you to keep the commandment" (1 Timothy 6:14) or *charge* the rich (1 Timothy 6:17). This word suggests directives from an authoritative source. It has roots in military practices.

In summary, both Old and New Testaments emphasize transmitting the truth or passing on the content of the faith. This is done through receiving and delivering, through preaching, teaching, exhorting, beseeching, and commanding. The New Testament also emphasizes the example of Jesus and the apostles in the learning process. This is the theme of the next chapter.

9

PROVIDING EXAMPLES OF DISCIPLESHIP

THE early church emphasized not only transmitting the truth, but also providing an *example*. Two Greek words, from which come English words like "imitate" and "mimic," illustrate this truth.

The first word is generally translated "to follow,"[44] especially an example: to *follow* an example (2 Thessalonians 3:9, KJV); and *follow* the example of leaders (Hebrews 13:7, KJV).

Paul uses the second word[45] a number of times: "be *imitators* of me" (1 Corinthians 4:16); *imitate* me as I follow Christ (1 Corinthians 11:1); the Thessalonians became *imitators* of Paul (1 Thessalonians 1:6); Paul instructed them to become "*imitators* of the churches of God in Christ Jesus which are in Judea" (1 Thessalonians 2:14).

Another word[46] is variously translated as "form," "example," or "model." A "*form* of doctrine" (Romans 6:17, KJV); things being *examples* (1 Corinthians 10:6, KJV); or events—happening as examples (1 Corinthians 10:11); believers had Paul as an *example* (Philippians 3:17); the churches "became an *example* to all the believers" (1 Thessalonians 1:7); Paul told Timothy to be an *example* of believers (1 Timothy 4:12); Titus was to be a *model* of good works (Titus 2:7); leaders were to be "*examples* to the flock" (1 Peter 5:3).

To provide an example is a unique New Testament educational emphasis. The place of the example in teaching is profoundly related to the words of Jesus, "Every one when he is fully taught will be like his teacher" (Luke 6:40). Jesus' understanding of teaching and learning assumes that the teacher provides a model for the learner.

The Father, a Model for the Son

Jesus said that the Father provided a model for Him, "The Son can do nothing of his own accord, but only what he sees the Father doing; for whatever he does, that the Son does likewise" (John 5:19).

"What the father does, the son does likewise" was a Jewish proverb. It grew out of the practice of a father's teaching his son a trade. The son learned by observing his father at work. In the process he became like his father. Jesus saw this teaching method in His own relationship with the Father. Jesus did only what He saw His Father doing. Jesus learned from His Father, as the Father provided a model.

Jesus frequently referred to His Father as a model. In John 5:20 Jesus said, "For the Father loves the Son, and shows him all that he himself is doing; and greater works than these will he show him, that you may marvel." Jesus' works were the works of the Father who sent Him (John 9:4). See also John 10:32, 37, 38.

Near the end of His ministry Jesus stressed that He had become like the Father! He said, "He who has seen me has seen the Father" (John 14:9).

Jesus, a Model for the Disciples

As the Father provided a model for the Son, so Jesus provided a model for His disciples. Jesus selected a group of twelve men to be *with Him* (Mark 3:14), to learn from His example. In Mark 1:16, 17; Luke 5:27, 28; and Mark 8:34-36, Jesus stressed "Follow Me!"

Jesus said that those who believe in Him will also do the works that He did (John 14:12). This paralleled the Father/Son relationship. Note also the repetition of the phrase, "greater works," as found in John 5:19, 20.

Jesus made clear that His way of working with disciples was that of providing an *example*. He said this when He washed His disciples' feet (John 13:15). The disciples were to love *as He loved* (John 15:12). And just as the Father sent Jesus, so

Jesus sent His disciples (John 20:21).

The early church recognized that Jesus provided a model for all of His disciples. Paul noted this many times in his epistles: believers are to welcome one another "*as Christ welcomed* you" (Romans 15:7); believers are to "walk in love, *as Christ* loved us" (Ephesians 5:2); believers are to have *the same mind* that was in Christ Jesus (Philippians 2:5); and believers are to forgive *as the Lord* has forgiven them (Colossians 3:13).

Peter also made the point that Jesus provided a model, "For to this you have been called, because Christ also suffered for you, leaving you *an example,* that you should follow in his steps. He committed no sin; no guile was found on his lips. When he was reviled, he did not revile in return; when he suffered, he did not threaten; but he trusted to him who judges justly" (1 Peter 2:21-23).

Paul Was a Model

Paul not only *transmitted* the *truth,* he also provided a *model* of discipleship: "learn by us" to live according to the Scripture (1 Corinthians 4:6); "be *imitators* of me" (1 Corinthians 4:16); "be *imitators* of me, as I am of Christ" (1 Corinthians 11:1); "join in *imitating* me, and mark those who so live as you have an *example* in us" (Philippians 3:17); "what you have *learned* and *received* and *heard* and *seen* in me, do" (Philippians 4:9). Note these four verbs. All have learning implications. The fourth refers to modeling, "What you have . . . seen in me."

Paul wrote about the kind of man he was in the

midst of the Thessalonians, and how they were to *imitate* him (1 Thessalonians 1:5-7); "remember . . . our behavior" (1 Thessalonians 2:9-12); "you ought to *imitate* us . . . to give you in our conduct an *example to imitate*" (2 Thessalonians 3:7-9).

Paul was a model for Timothy—you have observed my teaching, my conduct, my aim in life, my patience, my love, my steadfastness . . . continue in what you have learned . . . knowing from whom you learned it (2 Timothy 3:10, 14).

Teachers in the Church Are to Be Models

The Father provided a model for Jesus. Jesus provided a model for His disciples. Paul provided a model for believers. The New Testament also makes the point that teachers are to be models for learners. Timothy was to set the believers an *example* (1 Timothy 4:11-16); models were implied when Paul instructed Timothy to secure faithful men who would be able to teach others also (2 Timothy 2:2). Titus was to be "a *model* of good deeds" (Titus 2:7). Elders were to be an *example* to the flock (1 Peter 5:1-3). Believers were to consider the life of leaders and "imitate their faith" (Hebrews 13:7).

Modeling or setting an example fits well into a believers' church, the voluntary community of faithful people. Teaching is not a matter of commanding or telling people what to do. Rather it is inviting persons to follow teachers and leaders who live a life of discipleship. Such persons display and demonstrate for all to see what it is to be a follower of Jesus.

In Hebrews when the preacher called for faithfulness he said, "We desire each one of you to show the same earnestness in realizing the full assurance of hope until the end, so that you may not be sluggish, but imitators of those who through faith and patience inherit the promises" (Hebrews 6:11, 12).

All of this underscores the basic principle of Jesus, "Every one when he is fully taught will be like his teacher" (Luke 6:40).

This book was prepared to help church leaders study, discuss, and think through the teaching ministry for congregations in their time and place. In this process, the first step was to think about the congregation and how it provides a context for teaching/learning.

The next step was to turn to the New Testament to discover, on one hand, what was taught, and on the other, what teaching methods were used. With these backgrounds it is hoped that church leaders in many areas will span the centuries since the apostles and under the guidance of the Holy Spirit discern the shape of the teaching ministry for their time and place.

For many persons, the goal will be an understanding of the nature of the teaching ministry. For others, an additional goal will be the development of curriculum materials. In either case the purpose of this book is fulfilled when congregational leaders think seriously and deeply about the Lord's command to teach.

NOTES

1. See J. C. Wenger, *The Way to a New Life* (Herald Press, 1977). See also David A. Shank, "Toward an Understanding of Christian Conversion," *Mission Focus,* November 1976, Vol. V, No. 2.

2. See J. C. Wenger, *What Mennonites Believe* (Herald Press, 1977), p. 34.

3. For further development of this concept of the community and many others, see Norman C. Kraus, *The Community of the Spirit* (Eerdmans, 1974).

4. See John Driver, *Community and Commitment* (Herald Press, 1976), chapter 5; Marlin E. Miller, "The Gospel of Peace," *Mission Focus,* September 1977, Vol. VI, No. 1; and J. C. Wenger, *The Way of Peace* (Herald Press, 1977).

5. See Millard C. Lind, *Biblical Foundations for Chris-*

tian Worship (Herald Press, 1973).

6. λατρεία *(latria).* Note, the New Testament was originally written in Greek, and reference is made to Greek words to avoid missing the original meaning of the Scriptures.

7. προσκυνέω *(proskuneo).*

8. λατρεία *(latria).*

9. See Driver, chapter 4.

10. See Driver, chapter 6.

11. Exodus 19:6; Isaiah 61:6; 1 Peter 2:9; Revelation 1:6; 5:9, 10.

12. See J. C. Wenger, *Disciples of Jesus* (Herald Press, 1977).

13. See Marlin Jeschke, *Discipling the Brother* (Herald Press, 1972) also Driver, chapter 3.

14. See Paul M. Lederach, *The Spiritual Family and the Biological Family* (Herald Press, 1973).

15. τελειόω *(teleioo).*

16. διδάσκαλος *(didaskalos).*

17. μαθητής *(matheetees).*

18. διδάσκω *(didaskoo).*

19. διδάσκω *(didaskoo).*

20. μανθάνω *(manthanoo).*

21. μαθητής *(matheetees).*

22. παιδεία *(paidia).*

23. παιδεύω *(paiduoo).*

24. καταρτίζω *(katartizoo).*

25. διδαχή *(didakee).*

26. "You who were once slaves of sin have become obedient from the heart to the standard of teaching to which you were committed" (Romans 6:17).

27. διδασκαλία *(didaskalia).*

28. παράδοσις *(paradosis).*

29. παρακαταθήκη *(parakatatheekee).*

30. υγιαινόντων λόγων *(hygiainontoon logōn)*

31. παραλαμβάνω *(paralambanoo).*

32. παραδίδωμι *(paradidomi).*

33. παράδοσιν *(paradosin).*

34. κηρύσσω *(keerussoo).*

35. καταγγέλλω *(katangelloo).*

36. κηρύσσω-διδάσκω *(keerussoo-didaskoo).*

37. διδασκαλία *(didaskalia)*.
38. κηρύσσω *(keerussoo)*.
39. διαλέγομαι *(dialegomai)*.
40. ευαγγελίζω *(ūangelizoo)*.
41. λαλέω *(laleoo)*.
42. παρακαλέω *(parakaleoo)*.
43. παραγγέλλω *(parangelloo)*.
44. μιμέομαι *(mimeomai)*.
45. μιμητής *(mimeetees)*.
46. τύπος *(tupos)*.

Paul M. Lederach, Scottdale, Pennsylvania, served as executive director of *The Foundation Series,* a graded Sunday school series for children, preschool through grade eight. The curriculum is a cooperative effort of the Mennonite Church, the General Conference Mennonite Church, the Brethren in Christ Church, and the Church of the Brethren. Earlier he was director of the Congregational Literature Division of Mennonite Publishing House. He has spent nearly three decades in developing curriculum for congregations.

He studied at Goshen College (BA); Goshen Biblical Seminary (ThB); Eastern Baptist Theological Seminary (MRE); and at Southwestern Baptist Theological Seminary (DEd).

Among his published books are: *Learning to Teach, Reshaping the Teaching Ministry, Mennonite Youth,* and *Living with Threes, Fours, and Fives.* He has served the Mennonite Church as a minister and bishop, as president of the Mennonite Board of Education, and as a member of district conference executive committees. He is chairman of the task force on "Affirming Our Faith in Word and Deed" of the General Assembly of the Mennonite Church.

He married the former Mary K. Slagell in 1952. They are the parents of one son and three daughters.

MENNONITE FAITH SERIES

Edited by

Elizabeth Showalter and J. Allen Brubaker

This series of booklets sets forth briefly some of the major emphases of the New Testament as understood in the Anabaptist-Mennonite tradition—a faith which represents a cluster of beliefs somewhat in contrast with those of the major bodies of Christendom in the sixteenth century: Roman Catholic, Orthodox, Anglican, Lutheran, and Reformed.

The Mennonite Faith Series includes the following titles:

1. *How Mennonites Came to Be*, by J. C. Wenger
2. *What Mennonites Believe*, by J. C. Wenger
3. *The Way to a New Life*, by J. C. Wenger
4. *The Way of Peace*, by J. C. Wenger
5. *Disciples of Jesus*, by J. C. Wenger
6. *The Way of True Riches*, by Milo Kauffman
7. *Teaching in the Congregation*, by Paul M. Lederach

The booklets in this series are available in North America from:

HERALD PRESS
616 Walnut Avenue
Scottdale, PA 15683

or

HERALD PRESS
117 King Street, West
Kitchener, Ont. N2G 4M5

Overseas persons wanting additional copies or permission to translate should write to: MENNONITE BROADCASTS, INC., Box 1252, Harrisonburg, VA 22801.